Recruiting the Right Staff

Rowmark

Other Easy Step by Step Guides in the series include:

Telemarketing, Cold Calling & Appointment Making

Marketing

Building a Positive Media Profile

Stress and Time Management

Motivating Your Staff

Recruiting the Right Staff

Better Budgeting for your Business

Writing Advertising Copy

Writing Articles and Newsletters

Managing Change

Handling Confrontation

Being Positive and Staying Positive

Giving Confident Presentations

Successful Selling

All the above guides are available from:

Rowmark Limited
65 Rogers Mead
Hayling Island
Hampshire
England PO11 0PL
Telephone: 023 9246 1931
Fax: 023 9246 0574

E mail: enquiries@rowmark.co.uk
www.rowmark.co.uk

Easy Step by Step Guides

Recruiting the Right Staff

Chris Dukes

Rowmark

Published by Rowmark Limited
65 Rogers Mead
Hayling Island
Hampshire
England
PO11 0PL

ISBN 0 9 539856 1 X

Printed in Great Britain by RPM Reprographics Ltd. Chichester.

Note: The material contained in this book is set out in good
faith for general guidance and no liability can be accepted for
loss or expense incurred as a result of relying in particular
circumstances on statements made in this book.

Contents

About the Author

Chris Dukes has worked in the office environment for many years, and is presently the administrator for an Information Technology Project Office in a multi-national company. Present responsibilities include manpower allocation, production of time/budget statistics for management and operational planning purposes, and employment of both permanent and temporary staff in a project-oriented working environment.

Other interests include playing Irish folk music, caving, sailing, and diving.

Introduction

In these times of restructuring and downsizing everyone is expected to do not just his or her own job, but take on additional roles, some of which are new territory.

Whether recruitment is one of your many functions, a sporadic one, or simply new to you, there are two core concepts you need to take on board:

- Employing the right people is critical to the success of any business; and

- The total staff-base is probably your company's most expensive asset.

Recruitment is:

**purchasing an asset
for your company**

Appointing the wrong person can be expensive, not only in monetary terms, but also in terms of wasted time and energy. It can also lead to internal conflict, higher absenteeism and lost production time.

Recruitment, therefore, isn't simply about discovering ways to get hold of someone quickly to fill a gap; that would be a dangerously naïve thought process from someone in a position of responsibility.

Recruitment is about:

- an analysis of your company's needs, and

- most importantly, educating **yourself** to be able to fill that need to the most satisfactory conclusion for both company and prospective employee.

So what is there to know about recruitment?

It can't be difficult; after all, there are experts around to do that job for you. You could just pick up the telephone, call the nearest recruitment agency – believe me, they would be so pleased to hear from you – and then you just sit back and let them do their job.

Think again. Even if the logical end process is that you do pick up the telephone and ask the recruitment agency to act on your behalf, they're working for you – so if you don't know your exact requirements, how can you expect the agency to fill them satisfactorily?

It's easy to recruit.

It's not so easy to get it right.

How to use this guide

The guide is designed to be a reference tool to help perform the recruitment function, and thereafter to be an aide-mémoire:

- Read it to hone your awareness of what recruitment really means

- Read it to improve your knowledge of the processes involved

- Read it to consolidate your management of each recruitment project

- Get those who work with you, and those for whom you are recruiting, to read the guide to promote a unified approach to each recruitment project

- Use the guide to help you evaluate each vacancy on its own merit and recruit the best possible person to fulfil those requirements

- Read the guide more than once to help you remember the most important points.

What you will learn from this guide

This guide can't assess your particular recruitment needs for this vacancy at this time – only you can do that – but it will provide:

- a framework to constructive thought

- a template for subsequent action

- a guide to the pitfalls.

It will assist you to:

- think logically about your requirements

- formulate a plan of action

- proceed with your recruitment drive in the knowledge that you have a coherent end-game.

In short, it will put your recruitment cogs into gear.

Note:

To avoid confusion and the cumbersome usage of 'he or she' throughout the guide, the applicant or candidate will be referred to in the male gender. This should in no way prejudice your recruitment concepts.

Chapter one

Panic Stations

You're losing a valuable employee, you have a new project to cover, or your workload has increased and you simply need to recruit someone to shoulder some of the burden. Whatever the reason, you need to get someone in quickly. You haven't got time to muck about – after all, you're a very busy person, and time is money.

If this is your initial reaction, you're panicking. A panicking person doesn't make rational decisions.

Stop and think: getting it wrong is potentially far more costly in time, effort, frustration, and money.

Allow yourself space to think. If you're under pressure, prioritise your workload at the beginning of each morning. Deal with the things which are critical to your business, but don't let a sense of panic push you into making an impulsive decision.

What will happen if you wait one or two days before setting the employment train in motion? Will the world come to a grinding halt? Will the whole business fail? I doubt it.

> **Act
> – don't react.**

Immediate Action

Determine what level of employee you're seeking. If advanced skill-sets are not needed, then it's likely you may safely employ with minimal time loss, but the higher the level of employee, the more specific the skill-sets, the more time it may take to fill the vacancy successfully.

The initial thought process at this stage should be to categorise your prospective employee. What kind of person are you seeking to employ?

- **Non-skilled**: manual labour, junior office, shop assistant, nursing auxiliary

- **Semi-skilled**: particular skills or experience which may be relevant to the post, but don't necessarily involve high levels of education

- **Experienced**: particular skills relevant to the post backed by a professional qualification and/or levels of experience

- **Professional**: skills which have been honed by education or experience into increasingly specified targeted areas, usually backed by degree-level education or professional certification

- **Managerial** (or Director): as above, but backed by a suitable portfolio of successes.

You may very well be able to fill the unskilled vacancy or even the semi-skilled within a month, taking into consideration applicants who are constrained by the location of their home, children's school and spouse's work place. But even at this level, to employ more particularly you may have to take a week or month notice period into consideration.

So, we're already up to a two-month time-span; as a ball-park figure, you can add an extra month for each step up the scale for skilled, professional, and managerial positions, taking into consideration that the higher profile the job, the more notice the candidate may be required to give and the more particular you will be about the individual candidate. By the time you're at manager level (including project managers) you're likely to be looking at a timescale of not less than six months, and possibly a good deal more for a good, solid employment proposal.

After this initial and fairly superficial evaluation of type of employee, you have to ask yourself a simple question:

Can you or your business afford to wait that long?

If you can, go on and plan your recruitment campaign using the guidelines set out in the following chapters.

If not, you have two alternatives:

- recruit with immediate effect

- employ a contractor or temporary employee (temp) to tide you over.

Recruiting hastily

If you need to recruit hastily, you'll probably advertise via:

- Your local employment agency

- Your local newspaper

- Local advertising boards.

You can expect to find yourself recruiting either from those people who live locally and can give minimal notice, or those already out of work.

If people are looking for a local job because of social constraints, you need to ask yourself:

- Can they do the job? Just because they say they can doesn't mean it's true.

- If this person needs any job, under any circumstance, are they likely to have any interest in the business other than receiving a pay packet?

- Are they really suited to the job, or are you panic-buying from an available pool?

- If over-qualified for the post, are they likely to move on if a better job came along?

- Could they add any long-term benefit to your firm other than the present specific requirements?

- If the person is presently out of work, why?

Don't let any of these questions prejudice your evaluation. A person may not be lacking in skills or levels of commitment just because they're local, and they may have a very valid reason for being out of work. There are also some very positive aspects in employing from the local pool:

- The applicant may be readily available

- Community spirit is still strong in some catchment areas, and some people prefer to work for a local firm

- There will be no relocation fees to find

- A person who is content with his location for a variety of reasons, and shows no particular drive to find work out of the area may be more reliable as a long-term employee than one who is prepared to relocate

- You may find a person who doesn't quite meet your criteria, but who is keen and very well worth training up to higher standards.

Even if you're pressurised into employing at fairly short notice, you must still make an effort to understand the overall ethos and the kind of employee movement within the catchment area from which you're drawing.

The temporary solution

As an interim solution, there are plenty of contractors or temps out on the market today, at all ends of the work spectrum.

On the minus side:

- A contractor will usually be more expensive than an employee

- To a certain extent you have to take them at the face value of their CV or agent, though an interview is recommended.

On the plus side:

- You can contract to employ such a person for an agreed length of time with no other employment commitments – as long as you don't keep that contractor over a specified length of time doing exactly the same job, after which time they're deemed to be employed, and will gain the benefits of an employed person (contact the Inland Revenue for the relevant legislation)

- There's the possibility of renewing the contract if you fail to employ within the time limit, providing the contractor has not committed to other work

- People often see contract work as a way of gaining experience and proving themselves, and many contractors have successfully moved into full-time employment.

Note: unless you are clear about the legislation, it's wise to purchase your contractor requirement through a bona fide agency to avoid tax and Inland Revenue pitfalls.

In summary

- Reassess your own perceptions of your role as a recruitment officer. What does it really mean?

- From a recruitment point of view, think of your employees as company assets. If you get it wrong you could be purchasing a liability

- From the moment recruitment becomes a possibility take the time to evaluate your needs fully, and don't act until you've had time to think it through logically

- No matter how sudden or urgent your need to recruit, don't panic-buy. Getting it wrong could be far more costly in the long term than the perceived loss through delay

- If the need is urgent, recruitment is not necessarily the immediate solution. You can act to stabilise your situation by taking on temporary or contract staff.

Chapter two

Recruitment as a project

Don't make the mistake of viewing recruitment as an amorphous mass of work which will simply happen during the course of your working week. Instead, plan each new employment proposal as a project:

- Define the deliverables: what kind of employee you require, and when you ideally require to employ him

- Scope the costs: rates of pay, advertising and agency fees

- Evaluate the timescales: how soon, realistically, might you hope to achieve employment

- Plan the resources: your own and others' time.

Bear in mind that, during the design stages, a good project is a living, breathing beast which needs room for growth and flexibility. It will only begin to firm up and harden when the muscle has been added to the bare bones; but even then it must still be allowed to breathe.

In diving analogy there's a weary but rather important phrase:

> **Plan the dive
> and dive the plan**

However, when you make your dive plan, at the outset you allow a leeway of one-quarter of your proposed air usage as reserve, just in case you drift slightly deeper than you intended, get tangled in fishing line, or have to help a buddy out with air. At thirty metres under the water it's no good sticking to your original plan if your air is running out.

So perhaps this should read:

> **Plan the dive and dive
> the plan, but scope in
> a little flexibility
> because nothing ever
> truly goes to plan
> without a bit of luck**

So why have a plan? Because without it you're simply going with the tide, and somewhere along the way you'll get totally lost because there are plenty of sharks out there keen to help you do so.

It's also a very useful and visible little device for proving to your superiors that you're actually working on a solution to a problem.

The plan is simply a tool – your tool – a template to assist in a satisfactory conclusion without too many diversions along the way. Therefore, with each and every recruitment possibility, draw up as good a plan as is possible with the criteria you have at the moment, and be prepared to reassess the plan at each stage as new developments take place. In the fast-paced world we live in, even as planning is an essential process, inflexibility isn't an asset.

OK, so I need a plan. How do I do it?

Scoping the project

If you're with a department in a larger firm, you may be able to call on your Personnel Department or Public Relations Department to help you out, but even if you're trying to recruit for your department and have specialist needs, you still need to do the groundwork yourself. Don't undersell yourself. You're not simply an employment clerk who has to place an ad and sift the resultant CVs for the lucky winner; you're also a project manager, and a public relations officer, and the better you do this piece of planning work, the more successful your recruitment drive is likely to be.

The initial basis of a good plan is GOAL, SCOPE, and ASSUMPTIONS.

- In your case the goal will be the successful recruitment of an individual

- The scope is the work which needs to be performed in order to attain your goal, and which you will eventually place in a logical sequence

- The assumptions are your best estimate at costs and timescales, and which will eventually become firm milestones which indicate the successful completion of each task or group of tasks.

Firstly, itemise the easily definable criteria.

Basic:

- The job title

- Is it a new job or a replacement?

- What is the anticipated level of employment within the structure of your organisation?

- Who will this person report to?

- What is the ideal start date for a new employee?

Specific:

- Has a job specification (spec) been drawn up?

- Is there a fixed salary band, or has a remunerative package with benefits been compiled?

- Are there other benefits (pension plan, bonus schemes, relocation fees)?

Advertising:

- Is the job to be advertised locally or will it be run as a national campaign?

- Should it be put in the hands of a specialist agency – even a head-hunter agency?

Assessing Candidates:

- Who is qualified to assess the CVs, someone in house, or an external agent?

- Will a technical test be necessary?

- Will references be taken up?

Interviews and Offers:

- If there's an agent involved, will he do short-lists or first interviews?

- How many interviewees will you see?

- Who will conduct the in-house interviews?

- Will the interviewer have the authority to make an offer?

- Will more than one candidate be interviewed on a set date, and will a choice be made there and then, or should interviews be conducted as and when suitable candidates turn up?

- If an exceptional candidate has other commitments, how flexible are you prepared to be with timescales?

Don't assume anything. Do your groundwork. Check national salary bands for similar jobs with one of the consumer research bodies (such as Butlers), get appropriate periodicals and papers, and assess wage levels and packages being offered by other firms for similar employment options. Are yours adequate to attract the level of staff you need?

As the answers begin to unfold they will become three banks of information:

- Pure data: i.e. job profile, candidate type, qualifications needed, etc

- A list of people you need to involve in your plan, and their availability

- Constraints: such as time or money

The constraints of time will become your key milestones, around which the rest of your plan will probably have to fit. This is the point at which you really do need to start to organise your data. This is the point the plan begins to breathe.

But how can you organise the data?

Gantt charts

If you're familiar with Gantt Charts, and have a computer package which will run them, use it!

If you don't know about Gantt Charts, look at the very basic example which follows, and work out your own way to record information which will highlight the milestones and keep your project within a pre-specified timescale.

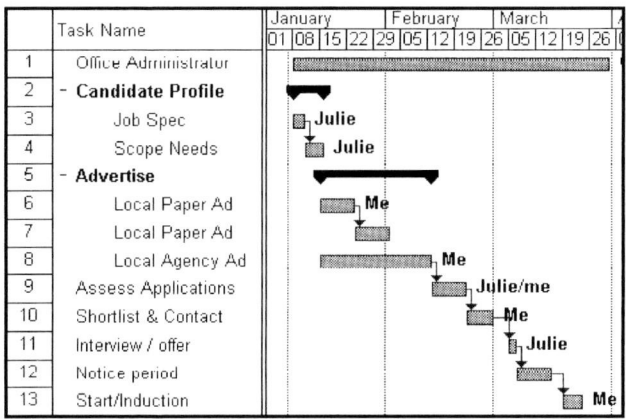

When beginning to organise your recruitment plan into a more structured shape you will probably discover some key milestones, i.e. dates which you cannot alter:

- A key manager is only available to do interviews at a certain date

- The previous job holder is leaving on Friday 10th and you would like to have someone in his place by Monday 13th

- You have a project which already has a start date, and you need the project manager by that date.

When you discover immutable dates, they will become the key milestones around which your plan will be formed. There is nothing like a challenge to get the grey cells working! If you do not have any crucial dates to contend with, the ideal starting date for your new employee is a good key milestone. Enter that, and work the rest of the plan backwards.

The job specification (spec)

The job spec is exactly as its name implies: a set of criteria which comprise the total responsibilities accorded to that post.

Set out the Job Spec as formally as you wish, giving the following information:

- Job title

- Reporting level within the firm

- Scope of job; include main responsibilities, but also add an ambiguous note to the effect that responsibilities may change according to the needs of the firm, to clear yourself of any post-employment legal nasties

- Type of person required, i.e. outgoing, good telephone manner, etc. Be careful not to add anything which could be construed as sexist, racist, ageist, etc. It's all right to say physical fitness is a necessity, say, if the employee is going to be humping lumps of iron around

- Levels of education required

- Previous experience required

- Do you require the applicant to complete an application form? As CVs are written in the applicant's favour, this can often be a good mechanism to establish a weighting criteria.

Selling the job

Do you only want to choose from the unemployed? There's an old adage: 'if you want to get a job done, ask a busy person'. This can be translated in employment terms to read: 'the good ones are likely to be already gainfully employed'. Ergo, you have to entice them away from their present employment:

- He's been in his job for a few years, and is vaguely thinking of moving on, looking for more responsibility and a salary increase.

- He's getting fed up with city life, and is thinking about moving to a nicer location with his family.

Don't forget you have to sell the vacancy. It's no good expecting the post to sell itself; part of your job is to make it attractive and entice the right level of candidate to apply. You have a fairly good idea of what you want by now, and have started doing a piece of work to try to sell this job. Don't assume the right person is out there desperately looking for work; it is not always the case. Your advertisement might just be the spur that will make an employed person think about moving on.

But hang on, you're saying, why do I need to sell it? Surely if someone wants a job, they'll apply for it anyway? And if they get it, they should be grateful! If you think this, check your ego. That is a very dangerous and outdated premise under which to begin your recruitment campaign.

If the candidate you choose to employ is unemployed in the first place, he will no doubt be grateful for a bit – but how long does grateful last, and what replaces it when it is gone?

Wouldn't keen, enthusiastic, reliable, career-minded go-getter sound better? If you want to attract quality staff, you need to forget 'grateful', and think more along the lines of having something to sell rather than being in the advantageous position of being able to offer charity. Make the position you are selling so attractive that the prospective candidate might choose to sell the old job to move in.

Selling your firm

You're not just selling the job; you're selling the firm, too. It's an inseparable package; the one comes with the other, and it's equally as important for the candidate to be comfortable with the type of employer he's approaching as visa versa.

Set out an outline of your firm, and the benefits of working for it. Even if you don't use it when advertising, it's a useful crib-sheet if someone telephones, and the various agents you may use will need a copy to help improve their targeting. It should contain the following information as a minimum:

- The firm's physical location. The name and address isn't always given if you're going through an agency; this ensures all applications go to that agency, and not directly to yourself. If you employ an agency, you have a legal obligation with regard to fees and, if you're not careful, you may find yourself paying those fees after having done the legwork yourself.

- The firm's business

- The firm's mission statement, ethos, or planned future direction

- A bit of the firm's background and history

- A clear identification of policy with regard to attitudes towards personnel, conditions, training, etc.

- The size of the firm, and whether it's part of a larger conglomerate.

Candidate Profile

For your own and your firm's use, it's often a good idea to get clear in your own mind the exact specification and type of person you wish to employ. This won't be intended for anyone outside your firm to view, but you should still avoid racist, sexist, ageist and other such remarks. Sensitive internal documents have been known to cause embarrassment in the wrong hands.

This set of predetermined criteria will help you to establish the validity of the CVs and applications you receive, and give yourself a more structured appraisal method for:

- Character type, general attitude

- Location issues

- Previous experience

- Personal motivation

- Reasons for moving job

- Personal Interests/hobbies

- Additional skills which could be of value to the firm

The criteria will obviously be defined by your own needs, and once you begin to specify them in your plan, you'll find they establish themselves with more clarity in your own mind.

If the nature of the vacancy allows you to be a little loose in your criteria you may need to make up a weighting for each bullet point, say marks from 1 - 5 (e.g. 5 being good, 1 being bad), and add them after the assessment to give an overview. This is an exceptionally good tool to establish an overall superiority if you have several candidates who seem to fit the bill, but who have different strengths and weaknesses.

Flexibility

At this point your plan is coming together, but keep your options open. It may well be that you started out with one idea but, by thinking it through and bouncing ideas against other colleagues, have ended up with a totally different concept of your requirements.

It may be that, having got this far in your employment plan, the pointers all indicate that this would be an ideal opportunity to look again at the possibility of taking on a contractor to fill this present requirement.

If so, be flexible and rework the plan.

In summary

- Treat each new recruitment proposal as a separate project

- Give yourself something to work with: set out a job specification and analyse the kind of person who would ideally fit the role

- Scope the project. Work out realistic objectives: timescales, costs, and deliverables

- Begin to think in terms of selling the idea to the candidates rather than assuming that you have something the candidates will fall over themselves to buy

- Don't think only in terms of employing from the pool of unemployed. It may be quick, but it may not be best. Think more in terms of recruiting from a smaller, more select group who meet your exact requirements and, ergo, may already be employed

- Once you have the bare bones of a plan and begin to flesh it out, don't set your objectives in stone. Keep yourself flexible enough to alter your objectives to meet changing requirements as your plan grows.

Chapter three

Contract labour

There's a definite case for contract labour in today's business world. Don't make the mistake of assuming contract labour is the last resort for a business in financial difficulties. For some businesses – not all – it can be hardcore business strategy to maintain a smaller nucleus of permanent staff and take on contract labour for specific projects and tasks. The labour directly costs more, but in real terms there are fewer overheads, and minimised redundancy obligations.

Also, don't make the mistake of perceiving contract employees to be the dregs from the employment pool. Many people now choose this as an employment option, and have skills which can command a high rate of remuneration. It should not be an assumption that contractors perform less well than employees; their future work depends on good relationships and end-of-contract assessments. However, a contractor is not an employee, and the interests of the business would be better safeguarded by having an employee in a position of responsibility monitor the performance of the contractor.

If you decide to go down this route, you'll need to establish relationships with one or more agencies, local or national, depending on your requirements.

Unfortunately, once you get into the contract market you'll be opening a can of worms. There's a very active grapevine out there, and the moment there's wind of a professional contract in the offing, every agency under the sun will call you. Believe me, there are hundreds.

Sole Agency

If you use a lot of contract staff, it can be beneficial to establish a sole agency agreement. You can bargain for better rates, but bear in mind that the agency may try to sell you the contractors they have on their books rather than shop around via other agencies.

They'll tell you that they can act as your agent and obtain staff from other sources but, although this may work to some degree, in my experience agencies are actually reluctant to pass work to another agency as the resultant commission or fee has to be further divided.

If you do choose a sole agency, be aware of contractual pitfalls. Allow your agent to have a lead time, say 5 or 10 working days to fulfil your requirements, after which you're at liberty to go elsewhere. Don't allow yourself to be hamstrung by a total sole agency agreement, and don't accept being told that this is normal. A contract is usually biased in the favour of the person presenting it, but most can be amended to mutual satisfaction before signing. Make it work for you, not against you.

Also in your agreement you need to specify working practice. It's fairly normal to request the agent to send you CVs of candidates short-listed by themselves, and for you to pick those you wish to interview from that short-list. I would expect to only receive maybe six CVs for any one contract, and would possibly choose only three to interview. If that isn't possible either you or the agent has not been clear enough in the specifications.

Don't allow your agency to flood you with CVs. If they do this, they're not working on your behalf.

Multiple v sole agencies

It's acceptable to have a preferred supplier list of maybe half a dozen agencies (P.S.L.) and, if this is so, be fairly ruthless in dampening the hopes of others that try to get a foot in the door. If you're not careful you'll end up on the telephone all day getting courtesy calls from the various agents determined to get on first-name terms.

If attempting to employ rather than obtain contract labour, however, you are probably going to be far more particular in your requirements, so even if the cold-calling representatives can seem a little pushy, maintain a professional attitude at all times.

Each agency can only offer you the staff they have on their books, and word of a vacancy does travel the grapevine; the candidate who is absolutely right for you may be on the list of someone you do not presently deal with. It would be a shame if you had previously upset them.

By using a P.S.L. you may be able to negotiate better rates but, again, be aware of contractual pitfalls. Always leave yourself room to manoeuvre if your P.S.L. agencies don't perform within a given length of time, or within a given advertising campaign.

In any event, you will probably be expected to agree to working terms and conditions before any CVs are sent to you – to safeguard the agent and their clients, so make yourself aware of these from the outset.

> **DO NOT SIGN ANY AGREEMENT OR CONTRACT WITHOUT THE ADVICE OF YOUR SOLICITOR**

With a multiple agency situation you have to be precise with your requirements and ruthless in assessing CVs. Each agency will try hard to get their candidates to in-house interview, hoping that in a face-to-face meeting you would simply like the person and agree to take them on.

Believe in your own assessments of CVs and do not be bullied into changing your mind; not only could you be interviewing for weeks, the exercise would probably only serve to reinforce the fact that your original assessment was correct.

In this instance you could request a maximum of, say, three CVs from each agent in the first instance, which will pressurise them into a much tighter screening of candidates on your behalf.

It may also be possible to prearrange with your agencies to perform first-level interviews on your behalf and at their own expense and only present for face-to-face interview those they would honestly choose for the job. This is not always a viable option, but remember you're the buyer, here, and in a position to bargain for better terms than will be initially offered.

Multiple agency pitfalls

Using multiple agencies, whether for contract or employment purposes, can sometimes lead to a particularly unpleasant hassle: which agency supplied the CV? It is similar to the problem of two or more estate agents supplying prospective purchasers with the same house details. They all want to receive the commission for a perceived piece of work.

In the same manner as a person trying to sell his house, a person looking for work will wish to get his CV seen by as many prospective clients as possible and, for him, sole agency is not necessarily the best option. So it is likely for a candidate to be on the books of several agencies at the same time; ergo, you may receive the same CV from more than one source.

When this occurs it can cause problems for the prospective employer, the agency, and the prospective employee.

There is no clear way to totally avoid this particular pitfall, but keeping clear records of which agency sent which CV on which date does help. If you use agencies regularly, it may even be wise to set up a database for this purpose; it is a useful tool if primed to inform you of duplications.

When a duplication is spotted, act immediately. Make both (or more) parties aware of the problem, and inform them whom you perceive to be representing this candidate. Be assertive, make the decision and hope everyone goes along with it. My initial response usually rests on the date of receipt of CV – first come, first served – but this is not always the moral choice, especially if the latter agency that sent the CV has been discussing the role in detail with the candidate and the former simply sent the CV out without doing the legwork.

If you are not interested in the applicant there is no problem, and no benefit to be gained by further investigative action. Don't waste valuable time on a pointless blame-seeking exercise.

If you are interested, however, the issue often has no clear and immediate resolution. Once the agencies scent a possible sale, they are very keen not to lose that commission. At this point they will very likely involve the candidate to enlist his support for their cause – which can either solve the problem immediately, or exacerbate it.

There are many reasons why duplications occur, and the answer is not always cut and dried:

- You may not notice the duplication to start with. There may be a spelling difference on the CV, in which case the 'no duplicates' function of your database will not pick up the discrepancy

- You may have already returned a call to one agency, only to have the other irately on the phone saying they sent it first, but by then the second one has then done all the interview arrangements and expects to get the placement fee

- You may also have the applicant tell you one agency sent his CV to you without his knowledge; not agency good practice, but it happens. Reputable agencies discuss each possible placement with the candidate before sending the CV to the client, but at the end of the day it's probably true to say the client does not care who gets the commission as long as he gets the job.

Though I have experienced each of these scenarios, I can't give you the answers here. Tackling such problems is part of your recruitment role, and it simply takes a little diplomacy to work the problem through. Searching for someone to blame is not constructive but, if you get to possible interview stage, it is wise to sort out the issue before making an offer. There is usually a sensible way forward for all concerned, even if the agencies have to split the commission.   It is in the agencies' interests as well as yours to come to an early solution. They will not wish to lose you as a customer.

Work permits

If you wish to recruit a foreign national as a permanent or contract employee, there will probably be no reason why you should not do so.

However, it is your responsibility as an employer to request a work permit or Visa from the Foreign and Commonwealth Office. You will find the address in the section on useful sources of further information at the back of the guide.

A job offer to a foreign national will always be dependent upon successfully securing such a Visa, and this should be made clear to the applicant.

Many people coming into the UK looking for work sign on with an agency in the first instance. If your contact is via an agency, do not assume that it is the job of the agency to provide this Visa for you; it cannot be obtained until a firm job offer has been made and the application for Visa presented by the prospective employer.

If you find yourself in such a position, contact the Foreign and Commonwealth Office for advice.

In summary

- Maintaining a smaller core of employees and using contract workers for specific projects is a possible solution to your needs – don't disregard the idea out of hand

- If you use contract staff, allow yourself the time to set up and maintain a good working relationship with the chosen agencies

- Interview possible agency staff with the same dedication you would give to permanent employees – they could affect your business adversely or otherwise

- Beware of contractual pitfalls with agencies. Do not sign any contracts or agreements without taking the advice of your solicitor

- Keep records of submissions from agencies – agency name, applicant's name, date, position applied for – but remember that confidentiality laws also cover candidates' CVs. If you choose to keep CVs, safeguard them

- If you wish to employ a foreign national, it is your responsibility as his prospective employer to obtain a work visa.

Chapter four

Advertising the vacancy

If careful consideration has still left you certain that you wish to employ rather than go down the contract route, you'll need to make a decision on how best to get the job out into the market place.

You have formulated your game plan, and the important thing is getting the ad out ASAP, and the chap you just spoke to on the telephone has this amazing special offer if you give him the advertisement to place immediately. Lucky he called, really. Why not go ahead? You know what you want now, and a deal's a deal, after all.

But what happens a day later when you realise:

- your hugely expensive ad is going out just when you have a week's holiday booked, or

- the in-house specialist you have chosen to assess the CVs isn't going to be available, and assures you he'd have informed you if you'd mentioned the escalated timescales.

> **Plan the work,**
> **work the plan**

Be decisive, but don't allow others to force hasty decisions upon you.

Where to advertise

You could recruit via the local job-shop, local newspapers, national newspapers, specialist publications, the Internet, or put your request in the hands of a recruitment agency or head-hunting agency. You may also choose multiple methods for strategic reasons, but whatever your final plan, you need to establish your criteria right at the outset.

One major consideration, of course will be price. Advertising isn't cheap and agencies are not cheap, so you have to weigh cost against gain. Dependent on the level of personnel you're trying to recruit, the recruitment campaign might be expensive, but getting it wrong could be catastrophic for your business.

To get a passably clear idea of how you wish to proceed, you'll need to explore various advertising avenues to get ideas, prices, and possible packages. When you make contact, don't discount the input from these people; they have experience which you, perhaps, don't have. However, be aware they're experts in pressure selling, and know all the blackmailer's tricks inside out. Until you're familiar with the market, DON'T agree to anything before seeing it in writing, thinking it through, and tossing the ideas around with a helpful colleague.

This is the point where you make the prospective advertiser or agent know you're not going to be brow-beaten, but that you're open to suggestion, your plan can be amended to suit both parties, and you are prepared to discuss to jointly formulate a sound proposal.

Flexibility is strength, but don't deceive yourself into thinking lack of a plan is flexibility in the extreme.

> **Without fail, an amorphous blob of work goes pear-shaped.**

As your recruitment plan begins to gel, you're less likely to be persuaded to agree to something on the spur of the moment. There's a time for quick decisions, but dealing with media representatives in any form isn't one of them.

So back to the research.

Hardcopy advertising

Which periodicals best suit your needs? Is there a specialist publication that caters for your specific business: Information Technology, Fashion Design, Engineering, Retailing, Management, etc., or will you use a national or local newspaper?

Most of these decisions will lie in the type of employee you're looking for, and will be directly linked to the remuneration you're offering. Local advertising is relatively cheap compared with national or specialist, but will bear limited success when seeking a high-profile candidate.

Another major consideration is how much work you want (or have time) to do. If you get the right agency it might cost, but it would take a whole burden of work away from you.

Browsing the various publications is a useful way of obtaining an overview of the buoyancy of the current market. It will inform you which skills are presently in demand, which other firms are seeking similar types of staff, and what remunerative packages are being offered for similar skills both in your area and nationally.

When you have done this research, reassess your criteria. Are you offering enough to attract the right person? If not, can you justify offering a better package? If you need to, rework your plan.

Local employment agencies

Again, this route depends very much on the level of skills you're seeking. It's a very successful way of recruiting unskilled, semi-skilled, office and manual labour, but don't expect to successfully recruit hard-playing professionals via this route.

Professional and managerial people don't consider themselves job-seekers. They're looking for the next rung in their own planned rise up the recruitment ladder. These people will sign on with accredited professional agencies, scan the professional and national media, or be head-hunted.

If there's a local firm they wish to work for it's quite usual for them to cold sell themselves to the firm in the course of self-advancement; but it's doubtful they will be registered with the local employment agency.

If you think the local employment agency can work for your needs, however, take the time to make a personal visit, or invite them to meet you in your own environment to give them a better overview of the company they're recruiting for on your behalf. It's always worth the effort in the long term to foster a good working relationship between yourself and the person normally on the other end of the recruitment phone.

Have your firm's portfolio with you; explain the ethos of your firm and the exact criteria for the post, right down to the character-type you're looking for. This will help the agency make value judgements on your behalf, and will minimise the time-wasting process of seeing unsuitable applicants. Make it clear that applications should be made only via the agency for the same reason.

> **If you use an agency, give them all the help you can to define the vacancy, but let them do the donkey work on your behalf. That's the service you're paying for in the long term.**

Specialist recruitment agencies

If the level of staff you wish to employ is in the skilled or managerial bracket, you may wish to put your vacancy in the hands of a specialist agency as well as, or instead of, using specialist publications.

Once again, it's up to you to do the research. Approach more than one possible agency, read their blurb, their credentials and their financial statements, and don't be afraid to make a Companies Search. A bona fide agency will be only too pleased to assist in this process in the hope of building up a good working relationship with you for the future, and won't think less of you for erring on the side of caution. There are agencies which spring up offering huge discounts and making outrageous promises in the hope of drumming up business, many of which don't make the grade, and disappear with the same rapidity.

Make yourself aware at the outset of the contractual details you're being offered. Agencies have a multitude of working practices, some more ethical than others, and all will be out to make as much money as possible from each appointment. It is, after all, how they earn their living.

No matter what you're told otherwise, contracts are never standard and can be varied to suit your needs

---

If you really like the ethos of the agency, but don't like their terms, bargain. They'll want to obtain your custom.

Each agency will have some particular hook to try to grab you with. Try to learn to recognise the hook and weigh it up against the bare bones of the business proposition. Take note of the following queries, but remember this list is not exhaustive.

Finance and Contract:

- Do you pay the agency a flat fee upon successful placement?

- Do you pay a percentage of one year of the applicant's salary upon successful placement?

- Do you pay a search fee even if no placement is eventually made?

- If they advertise on your behalf do you or they pay for the cost of advertising, or is it a shared cost?

- Are they asking for sole agency and, if so, are there penalties you should be aware of?

- Do you get a honeymoon period, i.e. if the candidate turns out to be unsuitable you get a refund of the placement fee or a percentage thereof?

Candidates:

- How well do they know their clients, i.e. do they hold personal interviews when taking them on their lists?

- Do they check their credentials or take them on trust?

- Will they agree to put forward only a specified number of candidates for consideration at any one time?

- Will they take up references and test professional and technical skill-sets on your behalf?

- Will they do first interviews on your behalf?

Multiple v sole agencies

Refer back to Chapter three. The arguments for sole versus multiple agencies apply whether you are recruiting or hiring.

Internet and online recruitment

This is a fairly new route for the discovery of skilled staff, most particularly Information Technology staff you might not be surprised to learn. It is, perhaps, not so relevant to unskilled labour at this time. However, as households and businesses are increasingly likely to have Internet access this is clearly the way forward into the recruitment future, but there are pitfalls. As the Internet is so 'placeless' you must be very clear about location (including country) and rates of pay, which vary tremendously in different geographical locations.

The Internet is a boom-town, a Klondike gold rush for anyone who wants to set up a business without huge financial outlay. There are many companies springing up offering Internet facilities of all kinds, including recruitment; some will make it, some won't.

It is, therefore, even more imperative in this particular arena that you satisfy yourself that you're dealing with a bona fide company. Check out the company, how big they are, how many staff they employ, where they're located, when they were inaugurated, and where they advertise for clients. Check out their working practice. Find out if a representative of the firm is willing to travel to meet with you.

Many will offer astoundingly good terms. No fee up front, a flat-rate placement fee etc., etc.

You get what you pay for

Recall the old adage above? Not necessarily true, but worth holding in the back of your mind. A good piece of work doesn't come free, and never has. In business, when being offered a deal which sounds too good to be true, it probably is. Experience is as invaluable a commodity in your agency as it is in the staff you choose to employ.

If the Internet agency simply posts your ad on their web page and redirects all applicants to you, as some do, your e-mail inbox may be inundated with unsuitable CVs; but they don't all operate in this manner by a long way. There are Internet recruitment sites which offer much the same service as the traditional agencies, but for each additional service they offer the price goes up accordingly.

It is also probably true to say most specialist agencies are steaming into the technological age and offering their own Internet recruitment solution alongside their more traditional services, and it would appear that the differences between the two are being rapidly eroded.

Form a partnership

Think long term. It's likely that this particular recruitment project isn't going to be the only one you handle. It would make good business sense to build up a working relationship with your chosen agencies or media, so that for future recruitment some of the underlying structure is already in place.

If you do this, allow the agency or media to keep in touch with you on a regular basis, as they'll wish to do. It may seem like an irritant during a busy day, especially if you're not actively recruiting, but it will help cement the relationship and escalate your next recruitment project when it pops up unexpectedly.

Put the plan into action

Only when you have assessed the market place, made your choice of media or partner in the plan, and have a structured timescale which agrees with all parties, including interview policies and times (see the next chapter), should you go ahead. Once your vacancy is on the market you will be proactively recruiting, and this is not the time to change your mind about any of the details.

You will need to have set time aside in your diary to read CVs, assess clients, deal with unexpected questions, reassure interested parties...

However long it has taken you to get this far, the speed and efficiency with which you conduct yourself at this time will be the window through which the agencies, advertising media and applicants view your firm.

In summary

- Though you will contact various agencies at this time, do not advertise the vacancy until the plan is finalised in all its detail

- Familiarise yourself with market buoyancy, and rates of pay in the skills you are seeking

- Gain an overview of the market place for the skills you wish to employ, both nationally and locally

- Assess the methods of purchasing these skills, whether you intend to draw from the pool of people actively seeking work, or whether you intend to advertise

- Listen to the advice of people in the trade, but be wary of the 'quick sale/hard sell' mentality of some advertising executives and agency staff

- Never agree to deals offered on the telephone which do not allow you space to incorporate them into your own employment strategy

Chapter five

Assessing the applicants

This must be done as quickly as possible. People seeking employment are not waiting for your response before applying to other likely positions, and two weeks down the line without hearing a word from you isn't going to impress them in any way about your organisation.

This is a time for being proactive. If you read a CV and like it, let that person be aware he is being considered, even by means of a holding letter, i.e.,

> Dear Candidate
>
> We are interested in your application for the post of [   ] and will be contacting you by [day] [month] with further details ...

If you send out a letter like this, make sure you don't promise a timescale you can't keep. A holding letter isn't an offer of anything at all, and your subsequent letter may very well be negative, but in the meantime it will have put you on a better footing with the candidate. There's nothing more frustrating to a job-hunter than sending out a keen application which results in a long silence.

Other than job applications coming in from local employment agencies for manual or non-specific office or shop functions, you'll probably have requested a letter with a CV, and perhaps a job application form.

Be aware, the complexity of CVs can vary enormously, depending on the individual's writing skills and the sort of advice they've received from the 'experts' who surround them. Some advice will be 'keep it concise', some will be 'detail every little asset, skill, and experience, the better to sell yourself'. Certain agencies even have their own CV format and persuade the people on their books to follow them, which doesn't help if you're trying to assess the applicant's ability to express himself.

So you need to be able to read between the lines. You need to quickly assess whether the applicant has:

• The skills you're seeking

• The level of experience necessary to handle the job, or the potential to do so

• Is in the right price bracket

• Is within commutable distance, or willing to relocate

• A positive reason for applying for this job.

Don't be afraid to write to an applicant and ask him to expand on certain areas of experience. This isn't indication of any kind of commitment on your part, but may serve to clarify things one way or the other.

Of course, intelligent people will give you the answers they know you want to hear, but experience will teach you little pointers, such as over-enthusiasm, or the wording of your advertisement quoted back at you.

Be ruthless. Sometimes your own reasons may not be easily defined, but if instinct tells you a candidate isn't right, he probably is not.

The applicant's letter should offer:

- A request to be considered for the job

- A good reason for wanting the job

- A sound overview of his character, including something personal about himself.

The CV should detail factual information, preferably in reverse-time order:

- Previous employment, including dates, which should be consecutive, and include periods of unemployment (make a point of checking for continuity, but don't assume the explanation will be negative)

- Higher education and professional certification, inclusive of 'A' level or NVQ attainments

- A paragraph on future aspirations which are work-related

- A paragraph on personal and leisure activities and attainments

---

Weighing up the pros and cons

Nothing is ever cut and dried. Though that perfect applicant is out there somewhere, he might not be applying for your vacancy.

When assessing your CVs, and along with the weighting document you have already drawn up as part of the job spec, it's useful to categorise the key skills/qualities indicators into those:

- You must have

- It would be nice to have

And don't forget to leave a blank field for:

- Additional skills or qualities the candidate possesses which would add value your team, perhaps in a way which you had not envisaged

---

Reading between the lines

Though he may opt to do so, the applicant isn't obliged to tell you personal information such as marital status, religion, ethnic origins or even health, unless it has relevance to the job itself.

However, without some hint of the character behind the business knowledge it's very difficult for an assessor to make an evaluated judgement, not so much on the level of skills as whether this person would fit in with the proposed work environment.

Hone your analytical skills, and don't allow yourself to be moved by personal detail or sentiment. An applicant who tries to use emotional blackmail to persuade you to employ is, by that very token, suspect. Keep your own criteria to hand. Remain detached from the applicant's needs; it's your company's needs which are paramount if you're to make a constructive, evaluated decision.

Learn to read between the lines as most applicants, though sparing with these details, will give an essence of themselves within the text – whether by design or accident.

For instance:

- If an applicant has a sense of humour he'll try to make you aware of this without labouring the point.

- Letters designed to make your heart bleed, or full of clever one-liners, are highly suspect

- If the candidate is open about marital status and personal detail, he's discreetly telling you he has nothing to hide, and will probably be equally as open in interview

- If you require someone to have excellent communication skills, lack of command of language will often betray itself in the letter, even if the applicant sought help with the CV

- If the applicant has moved job frequently it isn't necessarily a problem, but look out for an excess of excuses or allocation of blame

- However, if the applicant is presently out of work, it would be reasonable to expect him to say why he left the previous job.

This list could go on and on. Only you know the type of employee you're seeking, the type of environment this person would have to fit within, and the character type which would best suit your needs.

Just remember as you scan the letters and CVs that each and every applicant is an individual and a human being, and something of this will show in the application, often in ways which would be difficult to categorise.

Taking up references

In the event that references are required, it is usual practice to request one reference from a source provided by the applicant, the other being his last place of work. However, be aware that an employer, past or present, has no legal obligation to provide a reference at all. His only obligation should he choose to provide one, is to make sure it is fair.

At this stage you are in a position of some responsibility, and in the interests of the applicants' well-being, integrity, confidentiality, and plain common sense should govern your next actions: you should do nothing which would cause the applicant difficulty in his present employment.

References should NEVER be taken up until a job offer has been made and accepted. The applicant should be reminded at this point that the references would now be requested, and the offer of employment is made on the proviso that the references prove acceptable.

In any event, it is doubtful the resultant reference would serve to alter the decision you have already made. In the present climate of litigation, the reference will probably do little more than inform you where and when the applicant last worked, or is presently working, and in what capacity.

However, it's still an exercise which isn't entirely wasted, as confirmation of these facts would tend to indicate that other information on the CV is likely to be correct. The knowledge that references will be taken up also might help contain the applicants' inventiveness.

This means you must assume the applicant has been reasonably honest in his application, and your decision to take up references is, for the most part, a formality. By the time you reach this stage, you will have already decided you wish to employ this person.

Assessing technical skills

Although outright dishonesty can't be ruled out, most people wouldn't pretend to have technical skills they don't have. This would become obvious all too soon in an employment situation. But in the cause of financial self-advancement there is sometimes an inclination to stretch the truth, stretch oneself to reach a higher target, or simply to have greater self-faith than is justified.

Our drift journey of 1967 failed due to poor equipment and the sorry lack of skiing skills of some of the team, despite the glowing reports each had given of his skiing prowess when applying to join us. I made a mental note to personally check out people's professed skills in future and never again to take CV propaganda on trust.

Ranulph Fiennes

If the person you employ doesn't have ι
you thought he had, you can always gι
notice within the probationary period oι
basis, but the consequences may have alι
had a devastating effect on your business oι ιne
success of your project, never mind the length of
time it might take to find a replacement.

If a technical skill is required, and that skill is vital
to the vacancy, the chosen applicant can be
requested to be skills-tested before finalisation of
a firm offer of employment, either by someone in-
house qualified to do so, or by an external
professional body. If this is part of your plan,
making it clear to the agency at the outset might
prompt them to do a little more investigative work
on your behalf before sending the CV to you.

When Ranulph planned his subsequent ice-
bound adventure he did not make the same
mistake, but verified what he had been told:

> **I soon learned that many
> of the team had been
> economical with the
> truth when completing
> the initial skills
> questionnaire...**
>
> Ranulph Fiennes

If you don't have the means or knowledge to do a technical test, most recruitment agencies will be able to point you towards the correct professional body, or even arrange this on your behalf for a fee. Again, this may be a costly exercise, though probably not more expensive in real terms than discovering you have employed the wrong person.

Bear in mind it's worth adding on to any written offer of employment a clause which safeguards you, the employer, in the event of the employee's lack of ability to perform the function for which he has been employed. It's fairly acceptable to have a three-month trial period of employment, during which notice can be given if the employee fails to perform adequately; but do check out the relevant employment law with your solicitor.

Short-listing and contact

Once all the CVs have been assessed, and you have listed them in order of preference, the applicants or their agents must be contacted, but make sure you have your interview campaign plan fully constructed before doing so (see the next chapter).

At this stage, don't assume all the applicants you have chosen are still available and are eagerly waiting to be invited for interview. Some might have changed their minds or been offered another job. Some people even use applying for another job as a ruse to persuade their current employer to pay more money to keep them on, and your interest may simply be the catalyst to make this happen.

So proceed with your initial contact fairly dispassionately, display no overt enthusiasm for the applicant, but simply ask whether he's still available and interested in the vacancy. If he is, formally invite him to interview, giving details of where and when, and request confirmation of intention to attend.

In summary

- Only consider the needs of you and your firm at this time. The needs of the applicant are immaterial and should only bear weight if they further the application to you in some positive way

- Be proactive; respond as quickly as you can to the agent or applicant, whether positively or negatively

- If you think you need more time to make an evaluation, write holding letters to those people you wish to consider further

- Teach yourself to read between the lines to gain a deeper feel for the applicant's character

- If needed, use a weighting document to help make a deeper analysis of the CVs which interest you

- If you have any doubts, don't be afraid to request confirmation of technical skills

- Do NOT send for references before a job offer has been made and accepted.

Chapter six

Psychological profiling

Psychology is, very simply, the scientific study of the human mind and its functions, especially those affecting behaviour in a given context.

People in positions of responsibility where reactions in time of stress can be life-threatening – e.g. airline pilots or army officers – are subjected to rigorous testing to make sure they comply with character-trait templates. It has long been accepted in these elite circles that certain character-types can handle stress better than others. This is utilised fact, not fairy-tale.

As a recruitment officer you cannot fail to see the implications. These days it is no longer acceptable for someone to merely be good at their job; they are expected to wear the job like an overcoat, and it has to fit. A good character-to-job fit is as important as obtaining the correct qualifications or experience.

Increasingly, as businesses are restructured, and management hierarchies flattened, psychology is taking an ever-higher profile in the candidate selection process. There are fewer people taking on positions of greater stress and greater responsibility; and, as the responsibility level rises, so does the need to make sure the right candidate is in the right job.

This philosophy is inexorably filtering into all recruitment levels of the business world as the norm rather than the exception.

Understanding psychology

The basic character traits were classified into four groups by Hippocrates in 460 BC, and those classifications remain constant today. His discovery/premise of the 'four quadrants' of human nature was based on the observation that although the symptoms of various illnesses did not change much, the way people described them could vary tremendously. Once he had classified his four basic types, or humours (see below), the way he could expect various people to react to the same illnesses could be calculated to an astonishingly accurate degree.

Hippocrates' humours and their modern interpretations:

- Choleric: **D**ominant or driving

- Sanguine: **I**nspiring or influencing

- Phlegmatic: **S**upporting or reliable

- Melancholic: **C**oordinating or compliant

(Often referred to as **D I S C** characteristics in psychometric testing today).

Psychology then remained fairly static for hundreds of years, until the early 1900s, when it became a recognised science in its own right.

Jung took Hippocrates' four humours, replaced the terminology with his own and added additional yardsticks to them: extrovert and introvert. This now gave a measure of eight distinct character types. Jung's wheel gives a visible indication of these basic character types in today's language:

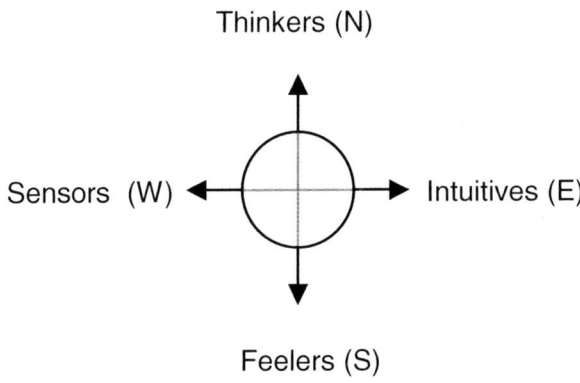

Thinkers (N)

Sensors (W) — Intuitives (E)

Feelers (S)

- **Thinkers** perceive the world by observation, internally digesting information

- **Feelers** want to get their hands on things to find out how they work

- **Sensors** make educated guesses but need to check everything out by tested methods

- **Intuitives** make educated guesses, and trust gut instinct.

Think of these characteristics as part of a compass, and the introvert/extrovert calculated as a magnetic variable. You will rarely find a true North or South; people are more complicated than that.

The different character traits, once classified, can either be strengths or weaknesses within a given scenario:

	Strengths	**Weakness**
D type	assertive	aggressive
	decisive	impatient
	direct	insensitive
	demanding	abrupt
I type	outgoing	disorganised
	friendly	irritating
	creative	keen to be liked
	spontaneous	fickle
S type	amiable	indecisive
	balanced	lacking focus
	people-orientated	passive
	compassionate	fence-sitter
C type	thorough	slow to respond
	accurate	bad with people
	objective	ignores feelings
	detached	uncommunicative

There are, of course, more and more divisions in the basic character traits, and as time goes by the psychometric tests are getting more tightly honed towards specific job functions.

But how do you discover these characteristics, and measure them?

It's called psychometric testing.

---

and on the subject of psychology...

The term psychopath relates to people whose defined characteristics are extreme, causing conflict between socially accepted and instinctive behavioural patterns.

People with psychopathic tendencies can reach high levels of responsibility in business as they can be single-minded and results-orientated, and have minimal social conscience!

Psychometric evaluation

The word 'test' is a misnomer. The tests cannot be perceived in any way to be passed or failed; they merely evaluate the psychological profile or basic character traits of an individual.

Basic character traits are a combination of genetic make-up and early social awareness. Though these characteristics may be further honed by lifestyle, social interaction and education, they will have been fairly well established in the infant years. An adult may have some control over his own destiny, even to the extent of altering behaviour patterns to suit a given situation, but the core stuff which makes a person an individual will remain constant, and the psychometric test sets out to determine those factors.

There are vastly differing emphases which organisations place upon the results of psychometric testing, but usage is increasing daily. I believe that in the foreseeable future this kind of testing – rightly or wrongly – will become a requisite for any and all employment. If this happens, it will possibly even filter down for use in careers development, ostensibly to assist young people target achievable careers at an early age, based on their individual character sets.

In establishing an individual's areas of strength the psychometric test is also discovering his suitability for certain job-types. It is usual for each person to be stronger in one character trait than another, and for that to have a huge (possibly subconscious) impact on both his own choice of career, and his ability to handle certain tasks.

It is the **overall combination** of required character types in their varying levels which provide the answer for the employer; e.g.:

The team-leader job might demand a dynamic, assertive individual, but if that assertiveness is not counterbalanced by, say, a level of sensitivity (requisite to HR or communication skills), that perceived strength on its own might prove to be an incredible weakness; for he will prove to be not so much leader as a loner.

There are two basic types of psychometric test:

The **ipsative test** requests the candidate to choose between two questions, i.e. have you got a flamboyant personality or a reserved personality? There will be a simple tick-the-relevant box response.

The **normative test** is where the questions are weighted, and the candidate has to tick the relevant box to establish in what quantity he believes he has each particular characteristic out of, say, 1 - 5.

The tests are formulated in such a way that the person being tested can complete the test quickly and easily, either by ringing letters or numbers, or ticking boxes. The test will not usually be timed, but the candidate will be requested to answer each question as quickly as possible, with as little thought as possible, in order to provide the instinctive, and therefore most honest response.

Because you have tick boxes, or yes/no answers, you have easily quantifiable set of responses which can then provide statistics. The various tests have differing ways of portraying the results, but most are visible, i.e. a graph of some kind.

And yes, to answer the sceptics, it is possible to cheat. Psychometric tests can be manipulated by those who are intelligent enough to do so, and have done their homework on the subject. And yes, there will always be a few bright sparks who will attempt do this.

Even though psychometric testing does assume a level of integrity from the participant, it will often have a built-in qualifier which will offer an indication of the candidate's need to impress rather than be totally honest; but there is no fail-safe lie-detector in the system. In recruitment there is always a level of intuitive guesswork going on, and you must set your own weighting criteria based on the results of the psychometric test, qualifications, experience, interview feedback, the choices of candidate available, and gut instinct.

The validity of psychometric testing

In any given employment situation the results of psychometric tests are, of course, meaningless if the characteristics most relevant for the fulfilment of that role have not first been charted. You're trying to find a round peg to put in the round hole; and the round hole, therefore, must have quantifiable dimensions which can be used as your benchmark.

The test should also be from a valuable and unbiased source. Beware of psychometric tests not produced, tried and tested by a reputable organisation.

If you choose to use psychometric testing in your capacity as recruitment officer, educate yourself fully on the kind of tests that are out there, and the kind of results you might expect to get from them.

Once that evaluation study has been completed, set your own boundaries. How much leeway will you allow yourself if the candidates don't fall exactly into your ideal psychological profile? At which margin will you decide to employ/not employ based on the results of these tests?

Never forget you are dealing with human beings. There has to be some elasticity; but, by the same token, if you – or your superiors – discover a real lack of faith in the results of the tests, you might as well throw them away and go back to CVs versus instinct.

There is an amount of speculation and scepticism about the veracity of these tests and, indeed, there are variables which can affect the results; but on the whole the results of a well-constructed test should give a fairly accurate indication of character traits, even taking stress etc. into consideration.

In any event, a level of 'human' flexibility should be taken into account when assessing the results. As I said earlier, these tests give an indication of levels of character traits, but do not offer definitive classifications of any one individuals whole psyche. The human mind is too complex a structure for it to be that simple.

But, be assured, psychometric testing has little to do with tea-leaves and crystal balls, and more to do with research by psychologists.

Which test?

I'm not going to try to point you at any specific test; it's up to you to discover what's on the market and to assess which are more compatible with your organisation and your needs. There are many tests out there, and more evolving daily. There are many sources of material:

- Run a search on the Internet

- Ask your local job centre or recruitment agency for a recommendation

- Check technical-specific organisations or unions for recommendations

- Does your recruitment agency already have a handle on tests specific to your areas of need?

- Check with your local library for sources

- Check with professional bodies, such as known examination boards and universities

You should have no difficulty in discovering the sources, but perhaps more difficulty in assessing which is the best for you. The following might help you to decide:

- Check with consumer bodies for research results in psychometric testing

- Check the advice given by the various exam bodies regarding the psychological needs-assessment of your vacancy

- Traditional paper tests can be time-consuming and open to error on the part of the assessor, especially if you are doing this during interview, or are time-constrained in some other way. If possible, use on-line or computerised tests; they produce instant results and leave little room for operator error

- Try the tests out on yourself and your colleagues to establish the user-friendly nature of the tests, and to get an idea of how long it would realistically take to complete

- Unless you are a qualified psychologist, do not try to produce your own psychometric test

And when you have chosen:

- Educate yourself fully on the tests you choose to use

- Do a 'control', i.e. test the same group of willing and trusted employees on the short-listed tests to

  - make sure you are reading the results consistently, and

- to assess the value of those results by analysing the manner in which your control group already perform/fit to the jobs they do.

When you interview:

- Make your candidates aware of the type of test you will be asking them to perform, and why. Take away the mystique

- For the most accurate results, instigate a rapport with your candidate before sitting him down to do the test, and set the test in a friendly, relaxed environment.

In summary

- Psychometric testing is not a test of intelligence or skills, but an assessment of an individual's inborn character traits

- Psychometric testing provides a means of fitting a person's psychological profile to the psychological profile of the vacancy – without which the test is meaningless in a recruitment situation

- In order to understand the validity of psychometric testing, educate yourself on the basic premise of psychology as it relates to character traits and job situations

- Carefully evaluate the available psychometric tests before choosing for your company; some are better than others

- When you have chosen, learn to use the test to its best advantage before unleashing it on an unwary applicant

Chapter seven

Planning the interview

As part of your overall plan you need to determine, prior to the interview, how the interview will be conducted.

- Will the interviewed person be one of several applying for the same job being interviewed on the same day; or will it be a sole interview each time a good CV is discovered, and likely to result in an immediate decision?

- Will there be a technical review or test before the interview (or subsequent to provisional offer)?

- Will the initial interview be made by a qualified person in the department, followed by a senior manager's assessment, or will the interview be conducted by a panel who then retire to consider the verdict?

- Will a secondary interview be requested in the likelihood that the applicant is of interest?

- Will the interviewer(s) have the authority to make a verbal offer, or will the applicant be told he'll be contacted within so many days?

All of the above are acceptable, mostly determined by the authority of the interviewer to make that decision on behalf of the firm, and the level of staff you're trying to employ. The more senior the position, the more necessary it is to get it absolutely right; ergo, the more time is needed for internal consultation and discussion.

If you haven't got the authority to make such decisions, who has? Will he make himself available on the date of interview? The important factor is to make all decisions about the interview process ahead of the interview date. Whatever your choices, make sure that the day of interview isn't going to turn into a fiasco for the interviewee. You can't afford to lose the ideal candidate through lack of organisation or forethought on your part.

You should also make the decision on whether you intend to reimburse travel expenses to interviewees, and prospective interviewees should be made aware of your policy in this respect before attending the interview.

Conducting the interview

When you begin the interview, be up front about the type of interview it's going to be. Make the interviewee aware at the outset whether it's a sole interview, whether there are several interviewees, whether a secondary interview will be necessary, and whether a job offer is likely to be made at the end of the interview, etc.

I can't stress enough that an interview is a two-way process, not a test of survival on the part of the applicant. There should be no spotlights, no one sitting behind the applicant firing awkward questions, trying to catch him out.

> **The applicant will also be interviewing you.**

The interview is a place in which you're not only the judge, you're also judged. It's a place where not only capability, but also humanity and instinct play an important a part. Decisions will be made by both parties in the subconscious as well as the conscious.

Interviews can be fairly traumatic, and people tend to hide themselves to a certain degree behind some kind of passive façade; but behind this, make no mistake, you're dealing with a real person with his own agenda. The interviewee may look passive, but will be judging the manner of your interview, deciding whether you're likely to be a reasonable employer, whether he likes you, and whether he thinks he can work with or for you.

Conducting yourself

There is, without a doubt, a pecking order in any business, usually accompanied by an applicable remuneration, but during interview isn't the time to crow about your own status. Your status will be betrayed by the fact that you're interviewing, and by the level at which you're employing, and needs no election campaign to prove it.

During interview you're not only making an important decision for your business, you're also the showcase for the ethos of your business. If the applicant sees you as a pompous idiot, he'll automatically assume that the business is populated by pompous idiots.

Be VERY, VERY careful to monitor your own ego during interview. It's so easy to slip into a superior mode: you, the interviewer, have the power to change the course of a person's destiny...

If you think this, you're deceiving yourself. You may be a Very Important Person, but betraying self-importance during this time will both expose the amateur in you, and give a very negative message to the applicant about his own importance.

> **Without exception,
> in the first few
> moments of an
> interview, evaluations
> will be formed**

There will always be an element of friction in an interview. People who have never met before not only have to learn as much as they can about each other in a short space of time, but also make an important decision based on that evaluation. As the interviewer, your first, and possibly most difficult task will be to set the tone of the interview.

Your body language should immediately promote an open and friendly atmosphere.

This won't be achieved if you're in the middle of a phone conversation when the applicant walks in, and you wave him importantly to a seat. This is really telling him how important you are, not how important he is, or how important the interview is.

Be available for the interviewee. Smile, walk forward, present your hand. If you're behind a desk, come out to welcome the applicant. If you bodge these first moments, the whole interview is probably biased unrecoverably against you.

What questions to ask

You have already decided this person can do the job, so during the interview you're merely:

- Verifying what you believe to be true about the applicant's claims

- Verifying decisions which must be made if you choose to make an offer and he chooses to accept, such as relocation, timescales, and remuneration

- Making an emotive decision as to whether this applicant's general character type will fit within your team and working environment.

Don't discount this last item; it's the single most important feature of the interview. If you choose wrongly, you could be bringing someone in who will absolutely disrupt the trust and camaraderie which already exists within your team. This point alone is a particularly good reason for having more than one member of the current team present at the interview.

What questions not to ask

You have an obligation by law to avoid discrimination. This means you can't request information on marital status, religion, childcare, personal problems, disabilities, etc., unless it has direct relation to the type of job, usually only in the social sector.

Every question you ask must be applicable to an applicant of either sex, any race or religion, and should disregard perceived disability.

Tip: when a particular question comes to mind, such as childminding if the applicant is a woman, or anticipated sick-leave if the applicant appears to be disabled, ask yourself whether you would ask these questions respectively of a man or an able-bodied person. If you wouldn't, the question is probably prejudiced.

Most of the people who already work for you have problems of some sort which will have a psychological impact on their ability to function: pending divorce, sickness of relatives, finances, etc., but this isn't your affair, and neither are the problems of any new employees you may choose to take on. It isn't for you to worm problems into the open and then decide whether you think the applicant can handle them. How people cope with child-minding, disabilities, religious or racial conundrums is their own affair.

Often, however, people will be keen to impart personal information of their own accord in order to further their application by dispelling unspoken fears, but if they don't it isn't your place to ask. Keep your questions to those related to the job and the applicant's ability to perform it.

At the end of the day, it's your decision whether to employ or not. That decision will be based on a whole heap of differing criteria, but must not, on any account, be based on perceived discrimination.

In summary

- Plan the interview beforehand: the manner of your interview, the people who will be interviewing the candidates, the levels of responsibility accorded to those people, and the financial implications for those attending interview

- Begin the interview with the right body language

- Have a specification sheet of key indicators to hand, and refer to it to keep the interview on track

- Be assertive, but not overbearing. Be organised, but flexible. Keep the interview on target, but allow time for pleasantries and observations; you never know what you might learn

- Do not ask prejudiced questions. Keep all questions directly related to the nature of the job and the candidate's ability to adequately perform it

- Allow the interviewee to interview you.

Chapter eight

Making an offer

So, having found your ideal candidate, you wish to make an offer.

You would be wise to speak personally to the candidate first, probably by telephone, suggesting you're interested in making an offer, and asking whether he is likely to accept if you do so. You might be disappointed at this stage for various reasons: the candidate by now might have simply decided he did not want the position, or he may have been offered sufficient incentive by a present employer not to move on.

If this happens, be positive. It's irritating but, if the candidate feels unsure, it's just as well to know this before employing him, only to have him hand in his notice two months down the line.

If the candidate is interested, but has his own criteria which need to be met, such as remuneration, relocation or benefits, this is the time to haggle and verbally agree the details between you.

Verbal contract

Whether you are dealing directly with the applicant or via the employment agency, before making the verbal offer of employment, be very confident you are making the right decision. Once you have made the verbal offer, and there has been verbal acceptance, both parties have an obligation to honour that agreement.

Though this will most likely be formalised in writing on both sides, there is no obligation to have a written contract. If you pulled out after a candidate had, say, given notice to another employer, you could be liable for the damage he has suffered.

In reality the employment offer or acceptance can still fall through at this stage for a variety of reasons but, should it do so, there must be agreement on both sides that this is the best way forward.

Confirmation of acceptance

You should then follow the verbal agreement with a letter to formalise the proposal, including wherever applicable:

- The proposed start date

- The covering clause that employment will be dependent on satisfactory responses from referees – bearing in mind that an employer has no obligation to provide a reference

- A covering clause either to formalise verbally agreed benefits or to suggest that a contract of employment covering these clauses will shortly be drafted

- All details of the contract or terms of employment.

You should also request the applicant to send acceptance of the position and the conditions set out in your letter.

The applicant, of course, might choose to add his own safeguards, such as: the appointment is accepted with the proviso that certain verbally agreed benefits (which he would probably detail) are contractually formalised.

In summary

- Speak to the prospective employee first to ask whether the candidate would be inclined to accept, if a formal job offer were made

- Finalise all employment details such as start dates and benefits

- If you are in agreement, only then make a formal, verbal offer

- Follow this up with a formal letter also detailing the conditions agreed between you

- Request formal, written confirmation.

Chapter nine

Contracts

Every employee is entitled to a contract of employment; any respectable employer would not fail to provide one. Although with some levels of employment the conditions might be non-negotiable, for a more senior level appointment a contract would be negotiated to reflect individual benefits and terms, to safeguard the position of both employer and employee.

If you're an established employer, you'll probably have a standard contract detailing legalities and codes of practice, with a schedule which may be altered to reflect the individual's particular package, including start date, remuneration, and benefits such as private health, car, or bonus schemes.

If you don't yet have such a contract, always employ a solicitor to draw up your standard terms. This will give rise to a one-off cost at the least, but is worth the expense. You may then copy and reuse this contract, simply altering the schedule to the satisfaction of both employer and employee.

A solicitor is not required to produce these subsequent contracts, but do be aware that, once signed by both parties, they are legal, binding documents.

If you do this, do not let your standard terms lapse. It would be advisable to request the solicitor to keep you abreast of any changes in employment law, and to reflect those changes in your standard contract from time to time.

The contract can't alter the employees' or employers' statutory rights by law, but will detail codes of practice within the firm, and formalise the accepted details and terms of the employment, including holidays, sickness, dismissal procedures, and termination clauses.

Expected length of employment

We live in a very flexible society these days. People move jobs to accompany a partner's career move, to forward their own career, or simply move job because they feel stale and need a new challenge or change of scenery.

There's no longer such a thing as a job for life, and both employee and employer have to accept the reality that each employment has a finite term. What that term is will depend very much upon the individual appointment; and for the employer, continually searching for employees to fill the same role can become a very frustrating task.

The employee/employer contract won't normally specify a term of employment but, in the event of taking on an employee in the upper managerial bracket, it would be acceptable to include an expected minimum level of employment, say, X years, perhaps with financial penalties and loss of bonuses if the employee hands in notice to terminate before that time.

Glass ceilings

Once a professional person is established in a firm it may be difficult for him to further his own game plan past a certain position, i.e. his own aspirations not being echoed by his present employers.

The term 'glass ceiling' is now widely accepted to apply to this phenomenon, and once the glass ceiling has been touched, for whatever reason, the only way the employee can forward his own long-term aims will be to move jobs.

It's likely that those employees trying to break through into upper managerial and director-level posts will experience this during the course of their career, and both employee and employer usually recognise when this occurs. Once an employee becomes dissatisfied with his situation, the only sensible solution for both parties is to let go and move on.

In summary

- Every employee has a right to a contract of employment

- Employment law will override any document produced or signed by employee and employer

- More senior level employees are usually in a position to negotiate an individual contract; be flexible

- Always use a solicitor to produce any document which you perceive to be contractual

- Request a degree of flexibility in the documents produced by your solicitor, in that you may reuse the copies of these documents on your firm's behalf with, say, an amendable schedule of dates, deliverables, and benefits

- Keep your standard terms and conditions of employment up-to-date

Chapter ten

It's not finished yet

So you have finally filled your vacancy. You can sit back with a sigh of relief, and go on to the next task.

But consider: if employing people costs a lot of time and effort and money, there is a lot to be said for keeping the employees you presently have contented. Quite often small perceptions of injustice or discontent which cause employees to desert are simply grudges or gripes that have been left to fester. Putting in place a process which allows opinions to be voiced without repercussion can do a lot to mitigate fermenting discontent.

Managing his employees' welfare is a major obligation on the part of any conscientious employer, and as a responsible employer you should, perhaps, discover this to be an essential part of your role.

Don't just show an employee to his job on the first day, expect him to find his own feet, and judge him by his level of success – be there for him from day one – and reinforce the lines of communication from time to time.

The Induction

You new employee will need a time to 'settle in' and understand his new role within the business. This can take some time, depending upon the complexity of the tasks he's been brought in to undertake and the ability of the employee to work his way fully into this role.

But wouldn't it be better for everyone if he was given some help at this stage? After all, the sooner he gets bedded in, the sooner he'll be fulfilling his true function, earning that money you're paying him. Set up your own induction process; once it's in place you can personalise it for each new employee.

Here are some ideas:

- Allocate your new employee a mentor – not necessarily someone of seniority, but someone who has been in the business for a while, knows where everything is and who's who.

- Produce a package of overall company information, such as

    - A history of the company

    - Personnel lists, telephone numbers

    - Organisational charts

    - Ground plans of your premises

- A copy of your published accounts

- Copies of company in-house policies regarding secrecy, usage of telephones, Internet, etc. (these may well form part of the contract)

- Organise induction meetings with key personnel in his own area of work

- Organise meetings with key personnel throughout the firm who can give an overview of various areas of the business your new employee might be involved with in the course of his work

- Prior to his engagement, make sure that all physical arrangements for his arrival have been met: tools, desk, chair, telephone, computer (including rights of access to the various mainframe applications or shared drives), parking space etc.

These are small tasks which produce a large result.

Planning for the future

Never assume that all your employees will stay with you just because you want them to. Life just isn't that easy.

One of the problems with working in recruitment areas is that it can be perceived in a very negative light. People are always handing their notice in just when you've knocked them into shape and they're at peak performance; but isn't that exactly when you should be expecting them to move on? When a job becomes easy, routine, the challenge is gone, and dissatisfaction begins to set in.

People don't often suddenly and unexpectedly leave their jobs. If you haven't seen the signs, you haven't been looking for them, which probably means you haven't got the systems in place to monitor for dissatisfaction.

Managing expectations

When we recruit, our needs are paramount. We're simply looking for the best person to fill the role we have. However, once your prospective candidate becomes your employee, once again you have a two-way process.

A business is an amorphous beast, and the job roles within it are never static; they are continually being altered by outside pressures such as political and financial markets and consumer needs.

Likewise, your employees' personal circumstances will fluctuate: the keen employee who used to work all hours suddenly finds himself with a young family or an ailing relative; an employee might outgrow his present situation and need to move on to a new challenge.

Getting the right staff is never the end of the story. There's a whole lot you can do to keep the staff you have, and to make yourself aware when an employee has reached the point where your business can no longer fill his needs.

To keep each employee functioning at his best those roles must be monitored and, if needed, altered to reflect the needs of both firm and individual. So, you have changing job functions and changing employee needs; how on earth can you monitor all that?

The simplest way to do this is to put into place yet another simple process: the personal review.

The personal review

If this is new to your business, market the idea before putting it into practice. It can be seen by employees and management in one of two ways:

- An assessment of performance.

  You'll be instigating a humiliating and traumatic process which every employee dreads, and which invariably ends with dissatisfaction and allocation of blame.

- A two way process with benefits.

  If either the firm's or the employee's needs have altered, now is the time for either party to be able to voice them in a friendly, constructive atmosphere.

Plan the process and produce a workable document which can be filled in on a yearly or twice-yearly basis by both parties. Your own business may dictate different needs, but here is an idea of some areas to cover:

- Re-evaluate the job description; is it still fair and valid? If not, you have some work to do

- Is the job title still valid? It's surprising how much this matters

- Evaluate training needs, and act on them

- Evaluate remuneration packages.

This is the time when you discover an employee might be adding so much more to your business than you realised, but you were so busy you hadn't really taken it into consideration. If so, reward the effort by bonus or salary increase; if you do not do so, your employee will go to someone who does; e.g. it might come to light that your employee knows a guy called Fred, who is doing the same job as he is, but getting more money. If you think you've done well to achieve this, and choose not to offer your employee the same rate as Fred, you're fooling yourself; don't be surprised or hurt when he hands in his notice.

Whatever the company spiel, loyalty towards an employee only runs as deep as current needs. Down-sizing, restructuring, and cost-cutting exercises usually mean people being made redundant, laid off. Employees and employers alike are usually aware that, in the firm's best interests, employees are ultimately expendable. Likewise, you have to accept at the end of the day the employee is only there for the money. Why else would he work for you? Loyalty? Love? Who're you kidding?

But, having put it into perspective, if you make sure he's a contented employee, he'll work well for you. If he isn't, he will not only work minimally, he could also be destructive.

If you make the personal review a two-way process in truth, your employee may well continue to grow with the firm, to consolidate his position with you rather than let discontent fester beneath the surface, unseen until he hands in his notice – or you have to get rid of him, by which time a lot of harm (the full depth of which you have yet to ascertain) may have been done.

If you discover your employee is really keen about a new area of expertise and has been training himself, but would benefit from a training course, suggest he does one. If you find an area of enthusiasm, even if you can't at first see a need for it – foster it! The goodwill you achieve will be immeasurable. It's not without good cause that 'goodwill' is given monetary value when assessing the assets of a firm. The same could be said for your employees.

This is the time to re-establish personal links between employee and employer, and a time for both to feel able to freely air niggles and gripes with a positive view to ironing them out; and if the end result is that you can't change the circumstances which make your employee unhappy, you can make an educated guess that he might sooner or later begin looking for another job.

Forewarned is forearmed.

The personal review is simply another tool to add to your managerial repertoire. It will never be able to change the overall ethos of your working environment. Teambuilding is not about power-play or about consolidating the pecking order; it is about communication. Breed an air of openness between workforce and management, and you will do much to minimise the secretive undercurrents of sniping and back-stabbing which can be so detrimental to the health of your working environment.

In summary

- Keeping your current employees contented is a sure way to reduce employment costs

- Introduce induction processes to ease your new employee into his role

- Keep yourself abreast of possible recruitment needs by monitoring the changing personnel needs of your company and the changing role of your employee

- And, most of all, be proactive in instigating an open door to communication; it is at the very root of good man-management.

Chapter eleven

Employment law

Though it has touched briefly on the legal matters to do with managing the employment process, this guide does not presume to educate you in your subsequent role as employer.

If your task is to undertake recruitment on behalf of your business, you will not be expected to understand the intricacies of law, nor should you try to. That's your solicitor's role.

However, you do have an obligation to make yourself aware of the law as it applies to you and your recruitment role; i.e. observing the laws which cover data protection, discrimination, and employment, and it might be a good idea to seek general advice from your solicitor on the level of your obligations in these areas.

If you're a small-business owner without the backing of a human resource or legal department, you may wish to educate yourself further prior to employing for the first time. I found the Which? Guide to Employment highly informative. It is both easy to read and understand, and also eschews legalese.

Keeping employee records

Employers who keep personal records on computer are obliged to register under the Data Protection Act.

You have a legal obligation to keep all personnel records, whether on software or paper, in a secure environment. This involves all information pertinent to their private lives, from medical records and personal reviews right down to address and telephone number. These records should not be made available to anyone in the business who does not have a direct business need to work with those records, i.e. a human resource leader or personnel manager.

Likewise, all CVs from job applicants should be securely filed; these are personal details which have been passed to you in your capacity as prospective employer, and those personal details may not be made available to any other party.

Once the appointment has been made, I'd recommend destroying applications – don't just throw them in a waste paper basket – as there's little to be gained from keeping them. It's unlikely the same applicants will apply again for the same post in the future but, if they do, the new CV will reflect more recent experience, and referring back to a person's old CV isn't a constructive action.

Statutes and Directives relevant to recruitment

There are U.K. Government and European statutes and directives relating to disability, discrimination, and data protection which can be obtained from or via the Open Government web site, or various other sources, some of which are detailed on the following pages. Obtain the latest versions, and keep yourself abreast of changes.

In summary

- Make yourself aware of the salient points of employment law as it applies to your recruitment role

- Do not keep applicants' CVs unless in a secure environment

- If you have no HR Department, take legal advice before recruiting.

Useful Sources of further information
(correct at time of going to print)

Open Government Web Site
www.open.gov.uk

Commission for Racial Equality
Elliot House
10/12 Allington Street
London
SW1E 5EH

Tel: 0207 8287022
Web: www.cre.gov.uk

Department of Trade and Industry
Publications Orderline
[Address as Employment Agency Standards]

Tel: 0870 1502500
Web: www.dti.gov.uk

The Data Protection Service
Wycliffe House
Water Lane
Wilmslow
Cheshire
SK9 5AF

Tel: 01625 545745
Web: www.dataprotection.gov.uk

Equal Opportunities Commission
Arndale House
Arndale Centre
Manchester
A4 3EQ

Tel: 0161 833 9244
Web: www.eoc.org.uk

Employment Agency Standards Office
Department of Trade and Industry
1 Victoria Street
London
SW1H 0ET

Tel: 0645 555105
Web: www.dti.gov.uk/er/agency.htm

Foreign and Commonwealth Office
Migration and VISA Division
1 Palace Street
London
SW1E 5HE

Tel: 0207 238 3858
Web: www.fco.gov.uk

Her Majesty's Stationery Office (HMSO)
St Crispins
Duke Street
Norwich
NR7 1PD

Tel: 0171 873 0011
Web: www.ukstate.com
       www.clicktso.com

Inland Revenue
- for local office use local phone directory

Job Centres and Recruitment Agencies
- for local offices use yellow pages

Acknowledgements

The Which? Guide to Employment by Ian Hunter
Beyond the Limits by Ranulph Fiennes,
published by Little, Brown & Company